MW00949020

inPromptu Journal

Random Thoughts Poetry Prompts

Offbeat Poet

inPromptu Journal: Random Thoughts Poetry Prompts

ISBN-13: 978-1072276494

Written & Created by: Offbeat Poet, Sherry Hale

Thank You for purchasing this book. Follow and tag Offbeat Poet to share your thoughts and work on social. Cheers to Creativity!

obeatpoet

Offbeat Poet
offbeatpoet.com

offbeatpoet

offbeatpoet

More Books
by Offbeat Poet

offbeatpoet1
#offbeatpoetry
to get featured

an exception to a rule

playing a game without all the pieces

not fitting in

taking the high road

saying goodbye

disappointing someone

grandma's cooking

making an exception

talking to a stranger

lighting a fire

accomplishing a goal

a solar eclipse

finding someone's wallet

a secret

defying gravity

something broken

being right

holding a grudge

something irreplaceable

feeling paranoid

losing a sense

something out of reach

breaking a rule

a bell ringing

a day that never ends

accidentally swallowing poison

sirens in the distance

perfection

burning your tongue

forgetting someone's name

opening a letter

living in the moment

letting go

an obsession

being criticized

falling in love

lipreading

feeling dizzy

clothes not fitting

your first car

waiting in line

unhealthy food

lying about your age

holding your breath

misreading social cues

deleting a friend request

the feeling before a sneeze

an awful date

laughing so hard you cry

dancing alone

Made in the USA
Columbia, SC
28 October 2020